Nickel And Dime
Your Way To Wealth

A Common Cents Guide To Investing

By
Deborah Owens

Caledonia Hill Press
Columbia, Maryland

*To Jason,
Dream Big!
Deborah Owens*

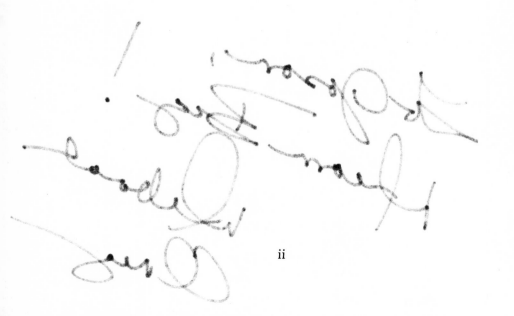

ii

NICKEL AND DIME
YOUR WAY TO WEALTH

THE "COMMON CENTS" GUIDE TO INVESTING
by DEBORAH OWENS

* Dream big! Act small!
* Small change reaps big rewards
* Change your outlook—Change your outcome

UPDATED SECOND EDITION

Owens Media Group LLC creates customized sales and marketing programs for Fortune 500 companies. They produce personal finance content for multimedia platforms; books, audio, workshop and seminars. OMG is the producer of "Real Money" personal finance radio show which airs on the NPR affiliate in Baltimore.

Copies of this book and others are available at
www.deborahowens.com
Owens Media Group LLC

Dedication

This book is dedicated to Mr. John.
Your generosity and spirit of optimism
are evidence of faith in action.
You have changed my life and countless others.
Thank you for paying it forward.

TABLE OF CONTENTS

INTRODUCTION

He regularly called in to the weekly public radio program that I host in Baltimore and changed my life. His name is Mr. John.

After two decades in the financial services industry as a stockbroker and vice president for a large mutual fund company, I wanted a change. The investment industry focused on "high net worth" clients; I wanted to make investing accessible to people of all income levels. So in 1996, I created the radio show "Real Money" with the purpose of helping "real people" take control of their finances. Each week since then, the program has devoted a full hour to an investment topic, featuring authors and financial experts, and taking questions from listeners on the air.

All the experts I interview tend to convey a recurring theme: *Invest for the long term and don't worry about short-term fads or market volatility.* Yet, in spite of this advice, listeners continued to call with excuses for why the experts' advice wouldn't work for them. After several years of hosting the program, I could no longer hide my frustration. The excuse that sent me over the edge was, "Investing is for the rich." My reply? "Investing is how you *get* rich." I could sense I was morphing into a talk show caricature. While the first five years were exciting and I looked forward to each broadcast, I was becoming the host who thought every question was dumb and wanted to hang up on callers. I prayed for patience to continue giving my listeners the encouragement and practical advice our show had been recognized for. Instinctively, I knew they would learn by example from others like them. Forget the experts. I needed to hear from real people, the kind of folks everyone could relate to. That's how the "Real Money, Real People" segments began.

These segments grew out of open phone nights when listeners called in with their questions or concerns about investing. I encouraged them to respond to callers if they'd had a similar experience and could share how they dealt with it. It was amazing to listen to "real people" share their experiences about finding financial advisors, or making their first investment and how it performed over time.

For several years, Mr. John called often with great suggestions. Typically, he made provocative investment recommendations such as "Miss Debbie, I think the listeners should invest in defense stocks." Each time he called, the studio telephone lines lit up. Because of that,

I asked him to be my guest on the first "Real Money, Real People" segment. He was flattered and extremely humble about his financial accomplishments. The only thing I knew about him was that he worked for a bank.

I began the interview with the question, "Mr. John, what was your first investment?"

He replied, "One of the first stocks I invested in was IBM. I scraped up the money to buy two shares."

"Do you still own IBM stock?"

"Yes," he said. "Those two shares have become 250 shares through the dividend reinvestment program."

"Wow. Who recommended that particular stock?" I asked.

"I purchased IBM in 1981 because I saw it mentioned on television and I knew it was a big company. The broker was upset that I was buying such a small amount, but he reduced his commission to 10 dollars— that was a big deal at the time."

When the phones kept ringing with questions for Mr. John, I knew the "Real Money, Real People" segment would be the answer to my prayers.

This interview with Mr. John also began a relationship that has inspired me to continue helping others become financially empowered. He has actually taught me more about building wealth than I learned from my formal training in the investment industry. In sharing

Mr. John's remarkable story, this book provides a roadmap for building wealth on *any* income. His story has put a face on financial empowerment and inspired thousands of people I've taught at workshops and conferences to take control of their financial future.

If Mr. John can do it, you can too.

NICKEL AND DIMING

Intrigued by Mr. John, I naturally wanted to know more about the types of investments he'd made over the years. So I offered to conduct a portfolio review, a process I used in my previous career as a financial advisor. Mr. John accepted my offer and invited me to his home.

Mr. John lives in a tree-lined neighborhood in one of Baltimore's famous row homes. The homes, designed by a renowned architect, have flagstone exteriors complemented by manicured landscaping. He greeted me at the door and introduced me to Delores, his wife of 36 years. Mr. John took great pride in showing me his home improvement projects in their modestly furnished home. In particular, he had paneled part of the living room and lamented that it still needed a few finishing touches.

The Portfolio Review

Settling down at the dining room table, I took out a

legal pad and calculator, and prepared to review Mr. John's portfolio, which discloses how someone's financial journey began and has progressed. The process reveals a lot about a person's investment experience—and I wanted to learn about his. He took out an accordion file and handed me statements from each of his main accounts. I wrote these headings on my legal pad: Date of Purchase, Security Description, Type of Account, and Market Value.

Mr. John's Non-retirement Accounts

We began by listing these four elements under the heading Non-retirement. Mr. John handed me the confirmation statement from his first purchase of IBM stock that he mentioned during his radio interview. He also showed me the dividend reinvestment statement from IBM. Then we listed 963 shares of Employer Bank, the stock from his employer that he purchased through payroll deduction. It had a current value of approximately $30,000. He also held several individual stocks in odd amounts: 113 shares of Duke Energy, 122 shares of Exxon, 5.33 shares of Bell South, and 54.38 shares of Colgate Palmolive. The reason for these odd amounts became clear to me later.

In addition to individual stocks, Mr. John had a number of mutual fund holdings. His first mutual fund investment was in the Fidelity Destiny II Fund, purchased through a broker. Through this contractual arrangement, he committed to invest $25 a month for 15 years. Although it carried a sales charge of 8.5 percent, it was now valued at more than $38,000.

He also purchased the no-load Fidelity Fund after dumping the Fidelity Magellan fund because of its recent lackluster performance. But he wasn't happy with his decision to sell the Magellan Fund. You see, portfolio manager Peter Lynch was one of his investment idols and although Mr. Lynch no longer managed the fund, Mr. John felt remorseful because it had been an exceptional performer in his portfolio. I also learned that I might have played a role in his decision to sell the fund. He had called into the radio show to ask my opinion and I suggested that it might have run its course. I was surprised to learn that he respected my analysis of the situation and recognized our radio show was providing listeners information they used in making investment decisions.

I noted that his investments were well diversified between stocks, mutual funds, and money market accounts. In fact, his portfolio mirrored those of many wealthy clients I had assisted throughout my career.

Mr. John's Retirement Accounts

Then we shifted to his Retirement portfolios. He'd invested a sizeable amount in his employer-sponsored

401(k) retirement plan, which held more shares of Employer Bank stock. He'd invested his annual IRA contributions in the Legg Mason Value and Special Investment Trust funds managed by Bill Miller, another outstanding portfolio manager. I later learned that Legg Mason had offices in Mr. John's employer's building, which helped explain why he initially invested his IRA contributions in its mutual funds. Convenience aside, Mr. John believed in "betting on the jockey," meaning investing in accounts with a portfolio manager who had a winning track record.

After reviewing his portfolio, I noticed that his IRAs were valued at more than his 401(k). This rarely happens because most people can contribute up to 15 percent of their salaries to their 401(k)s, and in many cases their employer matches a percentage. In comparison, at the time of Mr. John's portfolio review, the maximum contribution to IRAs was a few thousand dollars a year.

Mr. John's Investments for his Children

Next, we looked at the investments he'd made on behalf of his three children, who were all over 30 years old. Each child had shares of Exxon, Colgate Palmolive, Bell Atlantic (Verizon), and Lucent Technology. The number of shares in each stock varied from 7 to 75.

He had enrolled all of the accounts in Stock Dividend Reinvestment Programs, also known as DRIP plans. I asked Mr. John if his children knew about these investments and he said, "Yes. But I manage their accounts and hoped that one day they would follow my example."

How It Added Up

After listing and calculating the value of the holdings in his portfolio, I determined how his investments were allocated between stocks, bonds, and cash. This allowed me to research his portfolio's industry weightings and make sure he wasn't heavily exposed in a specific sector or company within his portfolio. Then I reviewed how his investments performed relative to similar investments over the same holding periods. Finally, I needed to determine if his portfolio met his objectives for future planning.

I realized Mr. John had no idea how much his overall portfolio was worth. After he pulled investment statements from every nook and cranny in his house, I used them to calculate the total value of his investment portfolio—$434,000. Not bad for a bank employee. But I still needed to know how much Mr. John earned at the bank and when he would retire to determine whether his portfolio would meet his objectives.

Nickel and Dimin' in Practice

I plunged in, asking, "Mr. John, how long before you can retire?"

"Oh, I plan on retiring in two years when I turn 65. That's when I'll collect social security," he said.

"What's your position at the bank and how much do you earn?" I asked.

"I'm the parking attendant and have been for 33 years. I earn just about $2,000 a month," he replied. "You see, I don't have much of an education. I was labeled a slow learner and dropped out of school in the eighth grade. That didn't stop me, though. I went to Frederick Douglas High School at night and finally earned my high school diploma. When I started working at the bank as a custodian, I earned $70 a week. I got a promotion to the parking attendant job and really enjoy it. I'm responsible for making sure the bank patrons can find a parking space when they visit the bank. I've had a great run."

I almost fell out of my chair. "How in the world were you able to save this much money as a parking attendant?" I asked.

"Nickel and dimin'," said Mr. John.

"Nickel and dimin'," I repeated. "What is nickel and dimin'?"

Mr. John explained, "There are two parts to "nickel and dimin'. There are nickel-and-dime *jobs* that pay $10 or $20 every week. That's what I earned from cleaning the Italian bakery shop and jewelry store, and landscaping outside the bridal shop across from the bank. The second part is nickel-and-dime *investments*. The $20 or $30 extra I earned each week added up to over $100 a month." And that's how he scraped up the first few hundred dollars to buy the IBM stock—investing the money from his nickel-and-dime jobs in blue chip stocks.

Now it all made sense. His shares of Baltimore Gas & Electric, IBM, and Colgate Palmolive had initially been purchased by nickel and dimin' and the odd numbers of shares of stock that he owned resulted from buying one or two shares at a time and reinvesting the dividends.

Access and a Mechanism

In his early years on that parking lot, a bank executive took Mr. John aside and told him that he couldn't go far with a limited education, and suggested he should save a few dollars toward his future. That was the first of many pieces of advice he received from his interactions with bank customers and employees. Mr. John took that advice to heart and acted on it.

Mr. John's accomplishments held extreme significance for me. Finally, someone could demonstrate that one's station in life did not determine what could be achieved.

You see, I had always believed that people simply

needed access and a mechanism for investing. It goes against the common belief in Middle America that investing is *for* the rich, not *how* to get rich. Early in my career, I remember inviting average folks into marbled, plush-carpeted offices and saw how many felt intimidated the environment. They associated it with being reserved for "rich people only." And while conducting a seminar at a university, a college graduate told me that investing was like gambling or "magic." Mr. John validated what I had always believed: Investing is not just *for* the rich; it's *how* you get rich!

How could I share that story through Mr. John's example? I didn't want to divulge too much for fear that I could jeopardize his anonymity. Of course, I should have known better than that. Mr. John was proud of what he had accomplished, yet he didn't brag or boast. Humility is his strong suit and he carried himself in that manner. In fact, many of his coworkers said he was a little too humble. Watching him greet and attend to customers in the parking stall reminded them of the days it was the only job available to a black man. But Mr. John didn't allow himself to dwell on how he might be perceived by other people. He had work to do and little time for stewing. So he encouraged me to tell his story in detail so others could learn how to "nickel and dime," too.

Nickel and Dimin'

Your station in life
does not determine what you can
achieve.
Investing is not for the rich;
it's how you get rich.

~ Nickel and Dime Your Way to Wealth ~

OUTLOOK DETERMINES OUTCOME

I had just arrived at the Department of Labor Headquarters in Washington, D.C. for an award ceremony honoring Mr. John. Although the building resembled a cement fortress on the outside, inside it was opulent with its marble foyer and hardwood-paneled rooms.

I was escorted to Mr. John's table where he was seated in a wheelchair, struggling to gain his composure. "Don't I look like a pitiful sight?" Mr. John asked, stricken by a case of gout the previous evening and unable to walk. His wife, daughter, and son also sat at the table. As I scanned the crowd—several hundred at least—I took note of the CEOs, scholars, and bureaucrats in attendance. They were all anticipating words of wisdom from the recipient of the first Osceola McCarty Super Saver Award.

Osceola McCarty, a washwoman from Mississippi, had accumulated $280,000 and donated $150,000 of it to the University of Southern Mississippi. The Department of Labor wanted to encourage Americans to save for their future, so it designed a Super Saver Award to be presented to someone who exemplified the same attributes of Ms. McCarty. A selection committee had combed the nation to identify someone worthy of accepting this award. Mr. John fit the requirement perfectly.

As we assembled on stage and the assistant secretary of the Department of Labor prepared to give Mr. John the award, I filled with emotion when I stepped forward to introduce Mr. John. With extreme pleasure, I told the story of how this man from humble beginnings faced insurmountable circumstances and succeeded in spite of them. Mr. John then shared experiences that had shaped his life and told how he achieved his financial goals. By the time he finished his story, many eyes watered and the room roared with applause.

We presented Mr. John with a crystal statue and he beamed with pride. He felt uncomfortable accepting this award while in a wheelchair because it was totally out of character for him—a man who proudly had held more than 10 nickel-and-dime jobs at one time. This was the first time his gout had flared up to such a crippling degree, probably from all the excitement.

When I had spoken to Mr. John the day before, he never let on that he was in pain and could barely walk. He simply anticipated the exciting day lying ahead. Mr. John knew how to make the best of any situation; nothing could ruin this day for him. At 63 years old, he exhibited behavior that I believe is the secret to his success in life: He expected a positive outcome.

Mr. John's Story

"Labeled a slow learner as a young child, I was left behind as my classmates went to high school," Mr. John began his story that day. "At 13 years old, I found my first part-time job bagging groceries in Baltimore's Lexington Market stalls. I made enough money to help my mother with the household expenses and pay some of the tuition for my siblings who attended Catholic school," he continued. Being labeled a slow learner didn't prevent Mr. John from completing high school. He worked during the day and attended Frederick Douglas high school at night. Certainly his positive outlook helped him earn a high school diploma.

"My wise mother insisted that I save and tithe a portion of my pay. These early influences in stewardship and faith helped me establish my work ethic and habit of savings at a young age. I remember my mother telling me, 'Save something from your pay every week.' I knew my future job opportunities weren't promising and the few dollars I earned at the open-air market wouldn't be enough to support a family. So I worked several odd jobs from cutting lawns to cleaning the homes of the Catholic teachers at the school I'd attended. As a single man, I made it work.

"All that changed when I met a girl named Delores at

a church function. Eventually we got married and I needed something steady to support my family. My mother helped me find a janitorial job at a bank that her employer had told her about."

Most people would have considered this 'port-a-job' position (as the janitorial position was called) menial. Mr. John viewed it as another open door. Eventually he was promoted to parking attendant, which presented him with the opportunity to interact with the bank's wealthy customers and the stockbrokers and executives who had offices in the building. He performed this role with pride and a sense of authority. Mr. John's outlook allowed him to see a bright future from that parking lot.

To this day, Mr. John's warm smile and helpful disposition leave a positive impression with everyone he meets. This extraordinary parking lot attendant presents himself with an air of dignity and humility. His dry-cleaned windbreaker, starched shirts, and pressed khakis show the pride he takes in his appearance. And woe to people who park their cars in the bank lot with ulterior motives. As they're asked to leave, they receive a lecture from the "Mayor of Pennsylvania Avenue" who admonishes them for disrespecting the bank's posted parking policies.

Attitude for Success

As I sat next to Mr. John at the award ceremony, I realized that his receiving the Osceola McCarty Super

Saver Award was destiny. You see, this book is not about how to get rich quick or how to make your fortune in the stock market. It's about the attitudes and behaviors needed to become successful in life. The first attitude is "outlook determines outcome."

Mr. John answered my prayers at a time when my frustration with my audiences' "outlook" was at an all-time high. My approach to "Real Money" had never been to provide the typical advice heard on television networks or read in newspapers. Instead, I likened myself to a skeptical cheerleader. I'd help demystify the technical jargon espoused by financial experts and provide listeners with the context to apply information to their own lives. Because of Mr. John, I realized that building wealth is an inside job. That meant to have listeners act on the information being presented on the show, I had to make a connection with their *hearts* as well as their heads. They needed to "see and feel" someone in circumstances similar to theirs for the message to be "real." Simply stated, their "outlooks" needed to be changed.

> Do you believe the future is bright? Or are you focused on the bad economic news that you constantly see and hear in the news media? There will always be negative events to focus on—but only if you *choose* to.

Recent History

Let's take a look at the events that have transpired since the 21st century began. While we were focused on Y2K and holding our computers responsible for ending the world, the stock market entered a period that compares to the stock market crash of 1929. The Internet/dot.com bubble burst and highflying technology stock prices plummeted, bringing the value of blue chip stocks down with them. We had just entered a recession.

In addition, in the early 2000s, Enron fell from grace and became synonymous with corporate scandal. Plus let's not forget the now-defunct Arthur Andersen accounting firm and subsequent downfall of MCI World Com, Adelphia, and Global Crossings. A host of other companies had to restate their earnings and the financial analysts who touted technology stocks were suspected of having ulterior profit motives of their own.

This sad state of affairs made seasoned investors run for cover. Given that a few years have passed and stocks have recovered, we realize that investors who sold their stocks did so at the absolute worst time. Money pouring out of mutual funds hit record bottom levels by the fall of 2001, the lowest point of the market's decline.

Making Lemonade

At the height of the technology bust, I asked Mr. John how he felt about his Lucent Technology stock losing 90 percent of its value. He replied, "I received Lucent shares as a result of the Baby Bells splitting up. They had a good run and I still think it's a good stock and will turn around in the future." That's what I call making lemonade out of lemons! I attribute his ability to stay the course with the fact that his conservative, diversified portfolio was not affected too negatively because Lucent made up only a small part of it. His blue chip stocks, including IBM and Exxon, declined, but not nearly as much as his technology stocks did. Indeed, Mr. John didn't follow the crowd in or out of technology stocks. Rather, he developed a different point of view from watching and listening to the bank's wealthy customers every day.

Stock Speculation

Twenty years ago, having just earned my securities license, my greatest fear was losing my clients' investment money on poorly selected stocks. In the early 1980s, personal computers gave way to all kinds of speculation. That's when I first invested in semi-conductor stocks like Seagate Technology and LSI Logic. In this arena, stocks commonly doubled in value in a month. Similar to the Internet bubble, everyone thought the economy was experiencing "a major shift from an industrial to a technological age." The personal computer would change everything.

In the early '80s, I would dream about the stock market crashing. Well, in 1983, I watched as those investments lost more than half of their value—and the rest is history. I actually received the outcome I'd expected. In fact, I felt relief as I sold those stocks and carried capital losses forward for years to come. Little did I know that 20 years later, LSI Logic and Seagate Technology would become leaders in their industries and purchased for a pretty penny by large companies. The personal computer *did* indeed change everything; it just didn't happen overnight. Needless to say, those few thousand dollars I'd invested in technology stock in the'80s would have been worth hundreds of thousands today. But I *expected* to lose money and therefore created my outcome.

In 1981, around the time I was investing in semi-conductor stocks, Mr. John found the nerve and the money to make his first investment. He had observed parking lot activity for more than a decade before he found the courage to approach a broker and make his first investment. He knew that he needed a lot of money to have a broker establish an account for him. Brokers often brag saying, "My clients need at least $100,000 before I'll give them advice." The fact that he didn't have much money didn't discourage him. He continued to ask questions and observe the wealthy customers at the bank. For example, when they needed a loan, they opened their safe-deposit boxes and used their stock as collateral. Mr. John had visualized visiting his private safe-deposit box where he would put 1,000 shares of stock that he would one day own. That represented wealth in his mind and he fully expected to own them. It's what wealthy people did, after all. I realized that, just as my outlook had created my outcome, so did his.

A Losing Lesson

My early experience as a broker influenced my future approach to investing. You see, if I had been as observant as Mr. John, I would have noticed that the veteran stockbrokers in my office steered clear of high-risk stocks. Most invested their clients' and personal fortunes in solid blue chip stocks. While I was investing in semi-conductor stocks, *they* invested in IBM and Procter & Gamble. Losing money investing in the stock market at the beginning of my career taught me an excellent lesson and established the conservative approach I take toward investing today. My outlook changed, too. Today, I fully expect my investments to create wealth over the long term.

Mr. John knew that he wouldn't become wealthy overnight. But he recognized that if he hung in there, he could be successful, too. Seeing the price of his IBM shares fluctuate in value and then watching those dividends buy more shares every quarter opened his eyes. My experience with investors has shown me most people can't duplicate Mr. John's success because they get in their own way, reacting emotionally to the rise and fall of the markets. I contend that the ability to build wealth doesn't require technical know-how. As Mr. John demonstrated, it requires an emotional intelligence that you can't learn in a book.

Think about how you react when the market goes down. Do you get scared and want to sell your stocks? When you see the growth in your investments, do you become so elated that you spend your profits? Respond in either manner and you will not experience success like Mr. John did. Those two shares of IBM purchased 20 years ago have grown to more than 250 shares because Mr. John controlled his emotions. He could have sold his shares out of fear or greed many times over.

I remember a time when the demise of IBM seemed imminent. In 1989, I had completed management training at an investment firm and was transferred to San Francisco shortly after the city had suffered a devastating earthquake. The recession of the early 1990s had just taken hold and jobs were scarce. IBM stock had been trading at over $100 a share, but by 1993, it was valued at only $13 a share.

My office was one block from IBM's headquarters on Market Street. I remember that several of the laid-off employees visited our investor center to rollover their retirement plans and many had several thousand shares of IBM stock. Their entire life savings had plummeted so much that these laid-off people had to sell their stock at rock-bottom prices to live until they found another job.

I asked Mr. John why he hadn't sold his stock when it lost so much of its value at this time. He said, "Ms. Debbie, I was trying to figure out how I could scrape up a few dollars to buy *more* shares of IBM. When I looked at my statement, all I saw was how many more shares I was able to buy with my dividends."

Mr. John was able to control any fear of loss by seeking opportunity rather than catastrophe. By keeping a positive outlook and focusing on accumulating small amounts over time, he was able to attain his goal of owning 1,000 shares of stock.

If you change the way you look at things, the things you look at change.

It worked for Mr. John and it will work for you, too!

<u>*Common Cents #1*</u>

<u>Outlook</u> <u>Deter</u>mines <u>Out</u> <u>Come</u>

If you change the way

you look at things,

The things you look at change.

Change your outlook,

Change your outcome,

Change your income.

~ A Common Cents Guide to Investing ~

~ Nickel and Dime Your Way to Wealth ~

HOW MONEY WORKS

"I didn't know enough to be afraid," Mr. John explained. He simply observed wealthy customers' behavior and followed suit. He listened to stockbrokers discuss the market and watched how the wealthy customers responded. They never panicked; instead, they added more stock certificates to their safe-deposit boxes. He listened to them discuss how many shares of a particular stock they owned and what type of dividend they could expect. Basically, Mr. John observed that wealthy people invested their money regardless of the ups and downs of the economy or the stock market.

Recent financial and corporate scandals of the early 2000s have shaken the confidence of average investors. They read their mutual fund and employee retirement plan statements and assume that their money has been standing still as if on a treadmill. It may appear that your money is standing still but, in fact, it is actually working on your behalf.

Throughout the years, I often asked Mr. John what he thought about the current state of the economy or stock market. In response, he changed the subject, opting to share his latest investment opportunity with me. By doing that, he showed he wasn't interested in the day-to-day gyrations of the market. Instead, he operated from the valuable observation he'd made in the bank's parking lot——that building wealth has *little* to do with ups and downs of the economy or the stock market. Building wealth has *everything* to do with investing. That's how wealthy people put their money to work. Working class people save their money in the bank; wealthy people invest their money in stocks and bonds.

Osceola's Savings

When I first heard the story of Osceola McCarty, after whom the Department of Labor's Super Saver Award was named, I wondered how her savings might have grown if she had invested in stocks. Here was a woman who worked from sunup to sundown washing and ironing clothes. She rarely left her home except to go shopping or make deposits at the bank. Earning only a few cents for cleaning each bundle of clothes certainly didn't leave much for saving.

While saving $280,000 represents no small feat, the comparison between Mr. John and Ms. McCarty indicates how money works. Mr. John represents a real-life example of what happens when people invest their money in stocks. By studying each of their stories, you can begin to understand the relationship between risk and return.

Risk is Relative

Gradually, Mr. John transferred his money from the bank to the stock market while Ms. McCarty continued to invest her money in savings accounts and certificates of deposits (CDs). Her money earned interest or "income." Over the years, those earnings compounded through the reinvestment of the interest "income," and accumulated to several thousand dollars.

Mr. John, on the other hand, put his money into stocks. He invested his money for "growth," as he anticipated the stock price to increase over the years. In addition, the stock he chose to invest in paid dividends— another form of income. It's through dividends that his two shares of IBM stock grew to more than 250 shares over a 20-year period.

Savings vs. Stock

Let's compare how these two types of assets perform over time. In the case of Mr. John, two shares of IBM that cost him $318 grew to be worth more than $30,000 over 20 years. If he had deposited his money in a savings account with its historical average of 4 percent interest, his $318 investment would be worth a mere $600 today.

In Ms. McCarty's case, she earned an average of 4

percent on her money in CDs. She was able to save more than $280,000 over her lifetime, and yet the return she realized was slightly above inflation. Although her principal or investment was not at risk, she had assumed "inflation risk."

> You have choices when deciding to invest your money. You have to determine your goal: growth, income, or a combination of the two?

> Whether you put your money to work for income or growth will depend on how much time you have and how much risk you are willing to take. Both Ms. McCarty and Mr. John invested their first nickels and dimes in the bank because it was safe. In effect, they lent their money to the bank, which paid them a fee in the form of interest.
>
> Depending on the type of investment you make, you assume one type of risk or another. Of course, there are tradeoffs in every investment you make. Understanding those tradeoffs can help you make better financial decisions.

The Inflation Factor

Ten years ago, a loaf of bread cost about $1 at the grocery store. Today, a low-priced loaf of bread costs

$2. That means in 10 years, a loaf of bread has doubled in price.

Has your income doubled in the past 10 years? Even if it has, your salary is simply standing still because the cost of covering all of your basic needs continues to increase. These needs include housing, automobiles, gasoline, natural gas, food—the list goes on and on. Because inflation has averaged 3 percent annually, your money has to earn interest above the rate of inflation to simply stay ahead of the game.

This stresses the importance of knowing how inflation affects your overall return. If your money can't buy as much as it once did, then you're risking your ability to maintain your standard of living. Again, risk is relative.

Putting Your Money to Work

By investing in IBM stock, Mr. John wanted to put his money to work for "growth," which means he wanted the value of the stock to rise or "grow" in value. Over the past 20 years, stocks have earned an annual rate of return of 10 percent. By putting his money to work in stocks, he had the potential to earn a 10 percent historical rate of return.

This is a major reason his portfolio grew to nearly a half million dollars. Clearly, his earnings grew far above the rate of inflation.

"Stock" Pile Your Money?

Although Mr. John's portfolio experienced several downturns in 20 years, his investment in IBM stock serves as a great example of how investing in big companies for the long term can build wealth in spite of the risk involved.

Why did Mr. John choose IBM stock? Because he learned it was a "blue chip" stock, which is simply a stock issued by a corporation that is both large and has been consistently profitable for several years. If you play poker, you know that the blue chip is the most valuable chip, which is where the term comes from.

A company issues stock initially to help finance its growth into the future. Its current revenues or profits might not be enough to finance its future growth. Rather than take out a loan from the bank or issue debt in the form of bonds, it issues stock and allows individuals to become part owners or "shareholders." By purchasing shares of the stock, people are able to share in the benefits of the company's growth.

A company's stock price usually reflects how well the company is performing. If the company does well and increases its profits, the price of the stock increases. If it's unprofitable, the stock's price falls to reflect the company's poor performance. While other factors, such as the economy and the overall stock market have an influence, the share price generally indicates how well a company is performing.

The Secret to Accumulating Wealth

Over the years, IBM's stock value has been up and down. In the mid-1980s, it lost more than 60 percent of its value and employees were laid off as the company restructured to stay competitive. Many shareholders sold their stock because they were afraid it wouldn't recover its value. Does this sound familiar? Even blue chip stocks hit bumps in the road, which is why it's sound advice to only invest money that you can afford to put at risk.

During that downturn, Mr. John continued to have his dividends reinvested in more shares of IBM. Instead of panicking, he felt overjoyed because those dividends could buy more shares at the declining price. In fact, he learned that volatility can be the greatest secret to accumulating wealth. Reinvesting the dividends helps investors deal with that volatility and experience the magic of compound growth, which Albert Einstein considered the "eighth wonder of the world." Where did Mr. John adopt the outlook that downturns in the market are opportunities to purchase more shares? From the wealthy bank patrons he got to know.

Stocks have historically outperformed any other type of investment over long periods of time, averaging between 10 and 12 percent annually for the past 70-plus years. Clearly, this result doesn't happen every year. The market might go up 20 percent one year and down 10 percent the next. That's why investing for the long term is essential.

Getting comfortable with this type of market risk is the most important lesson of all because your ability to continue to invest over the long term will determine your success.

Which type of investment you choose depends on your goal for the money and when you need access to your money. After answering these questions, you should be able to determine how much risk you can take. Understanding the difference between saving and investing is essential in order to master the art of building wealth. If you're accumulating money for a specific purpose such as purchasing a car or making a down payment on a home and you'll need access to your money within five years, then you "save" your money. If your purpose is for retirement funding or financial security and your time frame is more than five years, then it's wiser to "invest" your money. But before you invest, put money aside in case of emergency.

Common Cents #2

How Money Works

If you learn

How to put your money

to work for you,

eventually

you won't have to work at all.

~ Nickel and Dime Your Way to Wealth ~

DREAM BIG! ACT SMALL!

"When I watched the customers go to their safe-deposit boxes and take out their stock certificates, I made a goal that I would own 1,000 shares of stock," Mr. John had told me. Every day, he greeted the patrons of the bank with a warm smile and a kind word as they parked their cars on the lot. Sometimes they put important papers in their safe-deposit boxes; other times they spent an hour or two talking with their private bankers. Mr. John observed that when wealthy people needed to borrow money, they used their stock certificates as collateral for a loan. That helped him understand the financial security that owning stocks represented to him. He wanted the choices that stock ownership provided.

Wealthy vs. Working Class

Mr. John also noticed differences between the wealthy and working class. For example, wealthy people visit the bank at odd times of the month to deposit several checks, or interest payments from their bonds, or dividend checks from their stocks. Working class people deposit their paychecks either weekly or bi-weekly like clockwork. Retired working class people only visit the bank the first of the month to cash their social security checks. Wealthy retired customers visit the bank to deposit dividend checks from their stocks and redeem interest coupons from their bonds. Their money works for them so they don't have to work. Now that's financial security.

Harness Emotions to Meet Financial Dreams

I attribute Mr. John's financial success to connecting his emotional need for financial security to a specific goal. If building wealth were as simple as reading a book or attending a seminar, most Americans would be millionaires. But in order to achieve anything of significance, we need to have strong internal or emotional reasons for doing so. It's the fuel that propels us forward in the face of unforeseen obstacles or uncontrollable circumstances. In Mr. John's case, stock certificates represented much more than wealth to him. It represented independence.

What motivated Mr. John? I learned that, at the age of three, he had lived with his siblings in an orphanage for a few years when his mother suffered from tuberculosis. She eventually recovered and brought the family back together. "If it had not been for the charity of the Catholic Church, our lives would have been a lot worse," he recalled. He shared that memory with me when we visited a public school where he volunteers. This school was formerly the orphanage where he lived.

Achieving his dream of owning 1,000 shares of stock meant he could protect his children from having to experience a similar type of hardship. He wanted them to have options and choices. Clearly, his work ethic, faith, and outlook on life were shaped by his early childhood experiences.

My husband and I were the first to attend college in our families. We understood the value of a college education and wanted to make sure we could afford to send our children there, too. When our son Brandon was born, we invested in a pre-paid college tuition program. Michigan was one of the first states to offer a program allowing people to pay for tuition based on a projected cost in the future.

As a young married couple, we hadn't yet established any concrete financial goals, but we knew a college education meant a lot. Our need to provide our children with opportunities was the "internal" or emotional connection that motivated us to borrow $6,000 and buy in to a four-year college education program when our son was an infant. Paying the $200 monthly loan payment for three years put a dent in our budget, but by the time our son entered preschool, we had funded his four-year college education. We tackled saving for a four-year college education with $200 a month. It simply required three years of "acting small."

> If you want to achieve your financial dreams, begin by making an emotional connection. What financial dreams can you emotionally connect to? Harness its fuel to make your dreams a reality. Of course, dreaming alone won't make it happen.

Acting Small

I learned that Mr. John took the principle of "acting small" to another level. He first invested in two shares of IBM stock, with the intention of eventually owning 100 shares of IBM. After buying those first two shares of stock, he calculated what the dividend paid and signed up for the dividend reinvestment program. Then he added more nickel and dimes until he owned a "round lot" or 100 shares. I remember first questioning his approach thinking, "Is he for real?" until years later when he'd call into the radio show to remind us of his progress. I can't think of a better expression to sum up the mathematical process of "acting small."

Mr. John could relate to "acting small" because his mother taught him how to save something from his pay every week. When a fellow employee told him he could have money deducted out of his paycheck, he invested it in his employer's stock. The opportunity to invest in stock directly from his paycheck made a lot of sense, so he started having a few dollars deducted every week. When he received the first statement, he was thrilled at how easy this was. This experience of investing in his employer's stock purchase program opened his eyes to the fact that he didn't have to pay the broker a commission like he did when he purchased IBM stock.

At the same time, he discovered he could put something away every week in his employer's retirement plan. The same types of mutual funds that he had invested in with the broker were available through payroll deduction, again without brokerage fees. So he started investing very small amounts because he wanted to make he sure he could pay Catholic school tuition for his children and cover his bills. However, today, these initial small seeds put into his employer's 401(k) plan and stock purchase program account for more than 40 percent of his portfolio, far surpassing his goal of owning 1,000 shares of stock.

Although Mr. John had access to brokers who had offices in the same building as the bank where he worked, it took him more than 10 years before he summoned the courage to ask them for help. Mr. John was a product of his generation. No one in his family had ever invested in stock before, which is also true for many who called into my radio program and said that investing is only for rich people. Mr. John experienced that same anxiety. Initially, he didn't believe the brokers would take him seriously as an investor. The few hundred dollars he had to invest was a lot of money to him, but only peanuts to them.

> The most important factor in building wealth is time. Don't fall into the trap that many investors succumb to—waiting until they have enough money to invest. Begin with whatever amount you can. If it's saving your chump change at the bottom of your purse or nickels and dimes you throw on top of your dresser drawer, then so be it. The major key to your success is taking action, even if it's small.

The Benefit of Retirement Accounts

Remember when reviewing Mr. John's portfolio, I was perplexed that Mr. John's IRA accounts were worth more than his 401(k) accounts after 20 years? That's when I knew he was an unusual man. Rarely would IRA accounts be worth more than retirement accounts if a person worked for the same employer for more than 30 years, as he did. But, remember, his earnings were less than $20,000 a year during most of his employment (and 401(k) contributions are based on a percentage of earnings), whereas he could initially contribute $2,000 (now $4,000) annually to an IRA.

The question is: How did he find the money to contribute the maximum amount to his IRA? He earmarked income from specific "nickel and dime" jobs toward his IRA contributions. Some of his cleaning jobs paid less than $20 dollars a week. However, when he added the income together, he earned $200 or so a month. Those hundreds of dollars allowed him to contribute the maximum to his IRA accounts. He then invested those contributions into mutual funds and stocks, which grew to be worth more than his employer's 401(k) plan.

Many people make the mistake of contributing only the amount their employer will match in their retirement plans at work. For example, some employers offer to match, dollar-for-dollar, a percentage of the amount the employee contributes. Often people believe incorrectly that it doesn't make sense to contribute additional amounts. However, when you look at the principle of acting small, you see how small amounts can affect your savings over time. Couple that with the fact that your contributions to your employer-sponsored plan are tax deductible. Not only are you leaving potentially tens of thousands of dollars on the table, you're also paying more taxes. That means an additional $50 added to your employer plan could mean an extra $50,000 over 20 years!

Investing in very small amounts was an extremely difficult concept for me to comprehend in my first conversations with Mr. John. But after reviewing his portfolio, I saw the principle of "dreaming big and acting small" in living color. Also, Mr. John would not have achieved the same amount of success if he'd not invested in stocks. Small amounts really do add up. A college education, down payment on a home, or financial security is simply nickel and dimes over time. If Mr. John can do it, you can too!

It's easy to "act small." You can begin an investment program with as little as $10. However, $10 might not seem like it can make much of an impact. Can investing $10 or $20 at a time make a difference? Look no further than Mr. John. After all these years, Mr. John still buys one or two shares of stock at a time and calculates how many additional shares he will accumulate through the dividend reinvestment program. Dreaming big and acting small over a continuous period of time has been the secret to his success.

Common Cents #3

Dream Big! Act Small!

One nickel,

One dime;

One share of stock at a time!

~ Nickel and Dime Your Way to Wealth ~

YOU HAVE WHAT YOU NEED

"I couldn't take the money from my children's mouths," Mr. John had explained. Years ago, Mr. John knew that to make his first investment, he had to find an additional source of income. His parking attendant's salary didn't leave much left over after he paid his bills, so he took stock of what he *did* have: location. He looked down Pennsylvania Avenue and saw part-time opportunities in gardening and cleaning to supplement his salary. If he looked carefully, he saw that almost every business on Pennsylvania Avenue had a need he could fill. His story illustrates how easy it is to look everywhere for answers when the solution is staring at us.

Why Don't People Invest?

In a recent survey of middle-income households, more than 40 percent of Americans admitted they had saved nothing toward retirement. Why? Because lack of exposure and access to an investment professional or company can be major impediments to building wealth. Non-investors often feel shame and apprehension because they haven't been exposed to the investment markets and therefore don't feel comfortable asking others for help.

Another reason people don't invest is because discussions around money and investing are considered "taboo" in many cultures. Certainly this lack of understanding and access prevented Ms. McCarty from broadening her investment portfolio sooner than she did. I think it's also one of the causes for the limited participation in many employer-sponsored retirement plans. Remember, Mr. John worked close to brokers and bankers, gaining access to investment information, yet he still lingered for many years because of his ambivalence and his long-time belief that "investing is for the rich."

Common Excuses

Every week, people call my radio show with reasons why they can't invest. "It's too complicated; how do I know where to invest?" and "I don't have enough money" are their most frequently voiced concerns. Let's look at these excuses.

"It's Too Complicated"

If something seems too complicated, what's the remedy? Just begin to learn. Mr. John listened to the stockbrokers and the bank's customers while in the parking lot. They discussed different investments and he chatted them up to see what he could learn. He had access to a broker and got a sense of who might best fit his needs or give him a break because he was starting out with a little bit of money. Callers to my radio show often ask for a referral to a financial advisor or investment company. I suggest they use a similar approach to Mr. John's. No, I don't mean spending time in a parking lot, but rather chatting with financial advisors.

For example, in most communities, investment companies and financial advisors give free educational seminars. All they require is that attendees critique the event and provide names, addresses, and telephone numbers. Seminars like these are held in neutral, safe environments, allowing people to do research without making a commitment.

At these seminars, people also have an opportunity to observe the advisors and assess if they'd be interested in forming a relationship. Can the advisors explain financial concepts well? Are they polite? Would the personalities work well together? They can also meet others who already have a relationship with an advisor and provide firsthand experiences or referrals.

Attending seminars is an alternative approach to interviewing advisors in the captive environment of their offices and perhaps feeling pressured to make a commitment. Just thinking about going to an office and divulging their private financial information can make many people feel uncomfortable and stop them from getting advice.

Several investment companies allow people to open an account and invest online. (Visit www.smartmoney.com/brokers to learn what the top-ranked online investment companies are.) Of course, those new to investing may need someone to help assess the options and develop a financial plan.

> You'll find that investing isn't all that complicated as you begin to learn more about it.

"I Don't Have the Money to Invest"

When I see people talking on their cell phones, I

> To "find money," scrutinize your spending behavior and find ways to redirect your money. I call this "behaving your way to wealth." In order to "behave your way to wealth," simply change a habit, like buying magazines every week or coffee every day, and redirect the money to savings. The level of sacrifice you make depends on how badly you want your dream.
>
> What are you willing give up to "find" extra money for investments?

think, "There's an extra $100 a month that could be going into an IRA contribution." That would be one way to "find the money" to max out 401(k) plans or contribute the maximum amount to IRAs. As an example, Mr. John had a fondness for expensive silk ties but he gave up buying them in order to purchase his few shares of stock at a time.

Analyze Your Spending

The first time I analyzed my spending, I was surprised by how much I *really* spent on eating out and buying clothes, plus I decided my dry cleaning bill was too high. Building wealth is an inside job that requires mental preparation and making choices like I had to. One of the callers to my radio show said it well: "I simply got sick and tired of living paycheck to paycheck."

The American Savings Education Council distributes a wonderful calculator to help people "see" how changing spending habits can add up over time. One side of the calculator lists a number of items that most people spend their money on, such as candy, snacks, lunch, and lottery tickets. These items may not seem to cost much, but the calculator forces users to see how much they actually spend each day. The other side of the calculator demonstrates how those mere nickel and dimes add up to thousands of dollars over time. (Visit www.choose-tosave.org to request a calculator.)

Show Me the Money

The first step to finding "nickel and dimes" is to keep track of where your money goes. The process doesn't have to be overwhelming. A simple 3x5 notebook in your pocket is all you need. Write down every dime you spend and, at the end of the day, add up the total and look for patterns. Where is your money going? Are you spending your money eating out, or buying newspapers, magazines, and snacks? Once you identify your expenditures, you can begin to pinpoint the expendable "silk tie" in your budget.

If you don't have a budget, put making one on your priority "To Do" list and get started. Budgets provide another way to stay in control of your life. Any budget has fixed expenses, such as your mortgage, car note, insurance, and utilities. While you can sometimes spring money loose by renegotiating interest on loans, for example, it's discretionary expenses—groceries, clothing, entertainment, and gasoline—that wreak havoc on a budget. These discretionary expenses present opportunities to find money to invest.

When it comes to finding "nickel and dimes," a budget becomes your treasure map. With a few simple shifts in spending, you *can* find an extra $200 to invest each month.

I urge you to keep your adjustments realistic; don't

set yourself up for failure using a bare bones approach unless you are motivated and disciplined enough to do it. Rather than eliminate an activity altogether, find a low-cost alternative. For example, rent a pager for about $10 a month instead of a cell phone for $100. That way, you can decide whom to respond to and when. This will not only save you a lot of money, but it also will put you in control of your time.

Sample: Show Me the Money

Expense	Cost per Month	Alternative	Cost per Month	Savings
Cable TV	$50.00	Movie Rental (4 times)	$12.00	$38.00
Cell phone	$50.00	Pager	$10.00	$40.00
Health club	$60.00	Exercise equipment (one-time investment)	$100.00	$50.00
Lunch	$120.00	Brown bag 3 days	$48.00	$72.00
Totals	$280.00		$70.00	$210.00

Move Forward with a Plan

It's all about tradeoffs. Just as there's a tradeoff between risk and reward, the same holds true when spending less today to invest in dreams for tomorrow.

Here's what an extra $200 a month can accomplish:

The Power of Compounding Interest				
$200	**Ten Years**	**Fifteen Years**	**Twenty Years**	**Thirty Years**
8%	$36,000	$70,000	$118,000	$300,000
10%	$41,000	$84,000	$153,000	$455,000
12%	$46,000	$100,000	$199,000	$705,000

Some people don't have enough money every month to cover the basics or are hindered from finding money to invest. This challenge is real *and* it's also doable. Like Mr. John, it may be that they simply don't make enough to invest. The answer? Mr. John realized early on that after covering his expenses, he needed to "up his income" to start investing.

Once you've tracked your spending and established your budget, if you've determined there's no extra money to be found, you may need to boost your job skills and salary, start a side-business, or get a part-time job. There are many ways to earn extra money. Remember, you don't need that much to invest each month.

Creating Extra Income

Here are ways people have created extra income for themselves:

1. Increase Job Skills

Lifelong learning is an essential life skill. Changes in the marketplace happen with lightning speed, and a person's skill-set can rapidly become obsolete. Companies often train their employees for higher-paying positions.

> Does your company offer training? Talk with your supervisor to find out what you can do to be promoted. When you do it, remember to use at least part of your added income for investing—*after* contributing the maximum amount allowable to your 401(k).

Attaining higher education no longer requires attending school during the day or even on campus. Many universities now offer distance education and online learning. Although tuition has risen, it's easier than ever to fund education with scholarships, loans, and grants.

> For find out more about online learning and educational financing, visit www.petersons.com and www.finaid.org.

2. Start a Side Business

Many people increase their living by selling products like cosmetics, kitchenware, and household goods in their spare time.

3. Get a Part-time Job

Mr. John looked down the street and knew that each of those businesses could use his services. He also had a love for landscaping and took great pride in cleaning buildings. Happily, he found his "nickel and dime jobs" on the same street as the bank.

Follow Mr. John's example and earn your investment money doing something in your natural skill-set or passion. Many companies need part-time staff. Think about the businesses you frequent each week when you shop, bank, or work out. They already know you. Ask if they need part-time help. Who knows, maybe the gym where you work out will hire you and throw in a free membership. Then you can direct the money that you usually pay for membership toward your investment plan. The opportunity you need is right in front of you.

Many solutions won't require changing your lifestyle because you are already accustomed to living on your current income. For example, if your next pay raise is 5 percent and you're earning $50,000, that's an extra $2,500 a year that you can use to invest in a Roth IRA. According to the IRA chart, this allows you to save an additional $80,000 in 10 or 15 years—even more if you commit to investing your pay raises every year. Mr. John earned less than $25,000 a year at the time of his semi-retirement. He proves that you really do have what you need. If Mr. John can achieve financial security, you can too!

Common Cents #4

<u>You Have What You Need</u>

Having more money

will not solve problems.

Use what you have

to create what you want.

~ Nickel and Dime Your Way to Wealth ~

JUST SET IT AND FORGET IT

"He was pulling out statements from everywhere. I don't believe he knew how much his portfolio was worth." This is how I describe to my seminar audiences what happened at Mr. John's dining room table when I conducted his portfolio review.

Mr. John knew that financial security would take time and effort, but he set up his success when he set up a failsafe plan: automatic investment programs. "Put something away from your pay every week," his mother advised. The statements he'd haphazardly placed in the drawers of his dining room buffet were from dividend reinvestment programs that he'd not paid much attention to. This demonstrated another key to his success: The ability to "set it and forget it."

I laugh when people tell me they review their investments weekly. The so-called "active investors" display their portfolio holdings on their computer screens where they can review performance every day, hour, or minute. When Mr. John began investing 20 years ago, there was no CNBC, CNNfn, or 24-hour cable networks. The Dow Jones Industrial Average was never quoted on the evening newscast and few personal finance radio talk shows existed. Today, I believe watching your stock minute by minute can be hazardous to your wealth.

The media has made access to information about investing widely available to every household in America. It's great! People can have more information than ever before. On the other hand, this can be considered terrible if it causes people to make careless decisions. Every company will hit a bump in the road. For example, a company could introduce a new product that doesn't sell, or it doesn't meet its financial targets in a certain quarter. These events could cause a stock price to decline in the short term. Responding to these short-term developments has caused "in the know" investors to sell their stock when it didn't turn out to be a good long-term decision. After all, Apple Computer, IBM, and McDonald's have all experienced their stock prices decline, only to recover by correcting their marketing strategies.

Don't Get Pulled Off Course

It's important to avoid any "noise" that might pull you off course. Noise is everywhere and can easily distract you from achieving financial success. To build wealth successfully, behave like Mr. John and learn to "set it and forget it" rather than respond to opinions all around you.

"Noise" gets disguised in many different forms: market volatility, negative economic news, outside influences, and more. It can become a nightmare if investors respond to unforeseen circumstances by panicking or trying to time the market.

When to Invest

When it comes to investing, the only guarantee is that interest rates, the market, and the economy will go up and down. They always have and they always will. Indeed, not knowing exactly how the market will behave makes investing interesting. People often ask me, "When is the best time to invest?" My response is, "When you have the money." I say that because no one can predict the future. What's needed is a positive outlook and a basic understanding of how financial markets work.

Yet it's not enough to have a positive outlook. Though it's difficult, it's important to stay the course, especially if investments decline by more than 50 percent in one year. However, that actually occurs on paper; investors don't make or lose money until a transaction occurs. My conversation with Mr. John regarding IBM's precipitous fall in the early 1990s comes to mind. But that's when he said, "Ms. Debbie, I wish I could have bought more shares." After consulting with his broker and other investors to determine if he should sell his shares, he had no intention of selling the stock. His experience taught him that the dividends from IBM would allow him to purchase more shares because the price was much lower. Mr. John knew the benefits of setting it and forgetting it.

When to Sell

How do you know when to sell a stock? The answer comes from your research to determine if the fundamentals of the company have changed. In Mr. John's case, IBM had been a leader in computing. It had a phenomenal track record, had become too big and complacent, and needed new leadership. There was no scandal or fraud attached to its falling on hard times, therefore analysts believed it could recover. However, this wasn't the same situation with MCI WorldCom and Enron; they were trying to create revenues that didn't exist. The point is, get advice and conduct research before heading for the exit.

Choosing Investments

Other examples of "noise" include how highflying stocks and mutual funds are touted in the media or advertised in personal finance magazines and newspapers. Keep in mind that those high numbers displayed indicate *past* performance, not future performance. More often than not, the stocks that are the leaders in one year turn out to be the laggards the next.

Bet on the Jockey

For a company or a mutual fund to perform well, good management is necessary. This approach is called "betting on the jockey and not the horse." Lou Gerstner, the CEO hired to take on the daunting task of turning around IBM's fall from grace, had lots of practice "riding that horse." He had helped turn around RJR Nabisco and had headed American Express. Bill Miller, portfolio manager for the Legg Mason Value Trust fund and Bill Nygreen of the Oakmark fund family have consistently outperformed their peers because of their ability to identify and invest in strong-performing companies.

Look for the winning jockeys in today's market and your horse might have a better run. Whether they manage a company or a portfolio, your job is to find good managers with whom to invest your nickel and dimes. Their track record and proven performance can give you the confidence to "set it and forget it."

Index Funds

Another option is buying into an "index fund." An

index fund simply invests in all the companies of a market index, like the S&P 500 or Russell 5000 index. Because they don't need to hire a portfolio manager or financial analysts to conduct research, management fees are much lower than funds that are actively managed.

Statistics show that fewer than 80 percent of mutual funds outperform their benchmark indexes. Many financial advisors believe that diversifying investments into different types of index funds can be an excellent low-cost approach rather than investing in actively managed mutual funds. There is certainly nothing wrong with having a portion of your investments in index funds, which perform just as well as actively managed funds. In fact, they are often offered as options in employer-sponsored retirement plans.

The objective of the index fund is to mirror the performance of the index—no more, no less. Many financial advisors and investors believe that their steady returns combined with reduced expenses are a fair tradeoff for the potential higher returns realized in actively managed funds. I do recommend them in the right situations.

The Static from Advertising

A lot of other sophisticated "noise"—like that coming from television and shopping mall advertising—can hinder good investment decisions. "Buy me, buy me" is the refrain heard subliminally—the kind of "noise" that keeps us awake in the wee hours of the morning with "infomercial" promises of a svelte figure or a miraculous cooking apparatus. Many people dial the advertised 800-number and, before they can change their minds, the item arrives on their doorsteps. That's how well this advertising "noise" can work.

Companies use sophisticated marketing to encourage people to take action. They know the profiles of their prospective customers and the propensity they have to buy certain items. But beware. Advertising "noise" can cause us to sabotage our ability to invest wisely. An emergency such as a car breaking down or roof leaking can deplete our investments—and make it impossible to "set it and forget it."

Putting aside money for emergencies means you won't have to delete your cash reserve earmarked for investments. Be sure you do it!

"Set-Off" Points

Some people can go into a discount store or mall with a list and purchase exactly what they've written on their lists. For them, the "set-off" points like advertising music piped into the store don't influence what they buy that day. But others get set off easily and respond to stimuli around them. They tell themselves they deserve a new trinket or toy—and spare no expense. They become the marketers' ideal buyers because they easily get caught in their advertising traps.

The best antidote to overspending is to avoid the "noise." Affirm your commitment to save the money for investments *before* you purchase any items, especially big-ticket ones, at the mall. Better yet, speed past the mall entrance altogether.

Frequent Market Updates

For some people, following market updates and looking up share prices makes them nervous. Therefore, it makes sense to review quarterly statements instead of checking the price of funds or stocks daily in the media. Remember that the longer the period of performance is compared, the more accurate assessments can be made.

Looking at your investments daily or weekly and trying to determine performance is not based in reality. Take a much longer view. While "set it and forget it" does *not* mean you should ignore your portfolio, it *does* mean you need to give it time to grow automatically.

Emotional Investing in Cyberspace

It's great that the average person can invest using the Internet, but this unlimited accessibility can turn into another potential pitfall. When Mr. John has any concerns about his investments, he seeks advice from his broker and consults with other investors he knows and trusts. The true value of financial advisors is they can prevent investors from responding emotionally to outside influences. That's why it makes sense to establish a relationship with an investment professional to get help discerning fact from fiction and preventing poor decision-making.

You can still have the convenience of making transactions online while benefiting from having full-service investment relationships. Doing so allows you to reduce transaction costs when you don't use someone else's advice.

Using the "Noise" as an Advantage

Peter Lynch, the famous mutual fund portfolio manager, attributes one of his all-time greatest investments to an observation that his wife made while shopping at the grocery store (a form of noise). She noticed women were buying the "eggs" packaging that had panty hose in them. His research told him these stockings were made by Hanes, whose sales had increased significantly. With more women working in the 70s and 80s, they found that buying their personal wares in a grocery store was more convenient than having to go to a department store. Women are good at multi-tasking, which proved to be extremely profitable for the Fidelity Magellan fund. Have you noticed any products or services being advertised in the media? The companies who make the products might be a potential investment opportunity. Noise is everywhere and if you tune in carefully, you can be richly rewarded.

In the early 2000s, terrorist attacks and subsequent wars have caused the market to be more volatile and made many investors quite nervous. This "noise" has even made veteran investors uneasy. Yet Mr. John often finds opportunity in chaos and you can, too. For example, he called into the radio show and encouraged listeners to consider buying defense and security industry stocks. In fact, a year prior to the attacks that occurred on September 11, 2001, he suggested Martin Marietta as a stock to invest in through a dividend reinvestment program. Putting his money to work by investing it systematically and leaving it alone has been the secret to his success.

The "noise" in the marketplace will always exist, both in negative and positive ways. It comes down to how you choose to respond to that noise when making your investment decisions.

Common Cents #5

Just Set It and Forget It!

It's not about how much—

It's about for how long!

~ Nickel and Dime Your Way to Wealth ~

IT'S NEVER TOO LATE

"I had worked for the bank for almost 15 years before I got enough nerve to buy my first stock," Mr. John said, acknowledging that time got away from him. But he didn't allow his late start to determine his final destination.

If achieving financial security is our goal, then the decisions made today and going forward will determine our success. We need to face hard realities in the challenging economic environment that we live in. The days of working for one employer, retiring, and collecting a pension large enough to meet our needs for the rest of our lives are over. Mr. John proves that, regardless of our station in life, it's never too late to secure a financial future.

Also, because of medical and technological advances, people are living longer. Life expectancies will continue to increase. When the Social Security system was created 60 years ago, the life expectancy of a male was 63 years old. Quite frankly, the system was created with the intention of few people collecting full benefits for an extended period of time. But today, a man can expect to live 82 years on average and a woman almost 90. That's almost 20 years beyond the age of 67—the age which retirees can now collect full Social Security benefits. This means our money has to last a lot longer.

Add to that the fact that the average American has saved less than $10,000 for retirement. That means a lot of people will find themselves ill prepared financially. They'll be forced to make drastic changes in their lifestyles when they retire. To avoid this predicament, they're wise to follow Mr. John's example and take advantage of every opportunity to invest toward retirement—at any point in time!

> If you're a late-bloomer investor with retirement looming in the horizon, your choice becomes retiring later rather than sooner. You also have to make a conscious choice to commit more of your income to savings. What will you do?

Employer's Retirement Plan

While Mr. John's first investment was in an individual stock, when a co-worker told him he could invest in his employer's retirement plan, he was thrilled. Over the next 20 years, Mr. John was able to accumulate a sizable sum in his employer's plan.

I think it's best to invest in employers' retirement plans first—before any other investment. These plans allow us to gain an immediate tax deduction along with deferring taxes on the earnings. As an example, for every $100 put into this plan, the take-home pay is reduced by $60 on average. In addition, employers may match employee contributions dollar-for-dollar, 50 cents on the dollar, or another amount. That's free money! Consider employer-sponsored plans the first destination on the road to wealth.

Don't make the mistake of contributing only the amount that your employer will match. Rather, stretch your finances so you can contribute the maximum amount allowable. If you don't, you're leaving money on the table because you're not taking full advantage of the tax benefits. Remember, the more you make, the more Uncle Sam takes. By contributing the maximum amount to your 401(k), you reduce your taxable income. It may not seem like much, but an additional $50 a month could add up to tens of thousands of dollars in the long run. Nickels and dimes really do add up.

Retirement Plans for the Self-employed

For those who don't have an employer-sponsored

retirement plan, one can be created through an Individual Retirement Account (IRA), as explained in the next section. Self-employed people have even more options because of the number and types of retirement plans for the self-employed now available.

When Mr. John began his investment program 20 years ago, the self-employed retirement plan options were limited to a simplified employee pension plan (SEP-IRA) or a Keogh. Now people can establish their own personal 401(k) accounts and contribute over $40,000 a year, depending on their income.

In the past, these types of plans were cost-prohibitive because administration costs several thousand dollars annually. Now, a personal 401(k) can be set up for a few hundred dollars and provides access to hundreds of mutual funds or individual stocks. If Mr. John had the same opportunity, his SEP-IRAs would have been worth more than his employer-sponsored 401(k) plan.

Any income you earn that is not subject to withholding qualifies you to establish a self-employed retirement plan. If you play your cards right, you can have a 401(k), SEP-IRA, and a Roth IRA. Having many different baskets for your retirement savings is an excellent way to jumpstart your retirement savings.

With the passing of the Tax Relief Act of 2001, the contribution percentages increased from 15 percent to 25 percent. Clearly, the incentives to save for retirement are greater than ever before.

Individual Retirement Accounts

After fully contributing to an employer-sponsored plan, it's wise to invest in an Individual Retirement Account (IRA). There are two types: traditional IRA or Roth IRA. Which one you choose depends on your particular situation. My rule of thumb is if you can deduct the contribution, then invest in the regular IRA. Otherwise, the Roth IRA offers an unbeatable benefit of making tax-free withdrawals at the time of retirement. (Tax advisors can help determine the best choices.)

One of the first observations I made during Mr. John's portfolio review was that his IRA accounts were valued at more than his employer-sponsored plan. This is unusual because ideally people contribute a lot more to their employers' plans than to IRAs. The reason that Mr. John's IRA accounts are worth more is because his wages at the bank were extremely low.

If you've not taken full advantage of your employer retirement savings plans in the past, you, too, can leverage your other retirement savings options.

Saving for College vs. Retirement

Many parents are concerned about how to save for college and their retirement at the same time. Indeed, families have limited resources and must make difficult choices.

I believe the time to start saving for college is the day a child is born. That sounds good on paper but when families are paying a mortgage, car notes, day care, and school tuition, how many dollars are left for investing? Very few. Mr. John found a way to send all three of his children to Catholic school and paid off his mortgage. He did not, however, pay their college expenses because he couldn't afford them.

I suggest if a family has to choose between contributing to a retirement account versus a college savings fund, it's best to choose retirement savings. Here's why. A fully funded four-year college education is not a birthright. I believe there is nothing wrong with having young people work during the summer to save for their own college education and/or applying for financial aid. Hundreds of college loans and work-study programs are available to students from poor and middle-income families. The only debt that pays a proven return is financing college.

Far too often, I've seen the results of parents who've jeopardized their future for their children's college education. The best gift you can give your children is the ability to take care of yourself during your retirement years without becoming a financial burden to them. Plus the values your children can learn from investing in themselves are priceless.

Just Get Started

Ideally, the best time to begin a retirement savings program is when you're young. However, age has its advantages when it comes to saving for retirement. The Tax Relief Act of 2001 included several caveats. For example, the "retirement catch-up" provision makes it possible for workers age 50 or older to contribute additional money into their retirement plans. Late bloomers can now contribute $500 more into an IRA account or an additional $1,000 in their employer sponsored plans.

Our political leaders today recognize the challenges our country's existing Social Security system will face in light of the coming explosion of eligible retirees who will qualify for benefits. Specifically, fewer workers will be paying into the system and more retirees will be drawing from it, creating a crisis that will have to be solved. The solution, in my view, is to start putting those "nickel and dimes" into personal retirement plans.

Begin where you are. The more you can invest toward retirement, the greater your ultimate results will be. It doesn't matter what amount you begin with; it only matters that you start. Remember, it's not about how much; it's about for how long.

Think of the sacrifice Mr. John made when his income was less than $1,000 a month. "My wife thought I was throwing money away by investing," he said. In the early stages, you may not see much progress and it can seem like you're on a treadmill going nowhere. But start with nickels and dimes, and make a commitment to invest at least 10 percent of your earnings. As they increase, earmark all your pay raises and extra income toward your investments. When you do this, you're well on your way to building a retirement income.

Play Retirement Catch Up

The most important factor in experiencing the type of success Mr. John has is the ability to act as soon as possible. Conversely, the worst thing is doing nothing. Okay, it may require having a nickel-and-dime enterprise and working for more years. But don't allow panic and regret to paralyze you. Instead, follow in Mr. John's footsteps.

It's possible to play retirement catch up, winning by leveraging our talents and taking advantage of opportunities. It also requires acting small—even just saving $25 a week or $100 a month and contributing to employer-sponsored plans and/or starting an IRA.

If you don't play the savings and investment game, you can't win.

Start with what's affordable now and increase the amounts from there. Remember, money can't buy time; it's never too late to start.

<u>Common Cents #6</u>

<u>It's Never Too Late</u>

Begin where you are!

If not now, when?

~ A Common Cents Guide to Investing ~

Pay It Forward

"You have a limited education and you won't go far working at this bank," a bank executive once told Mr. John as he took him aside and encouraged him to invest his money. He too, had been labeled a "slow learner" as a child and had overcome his learning disability. He "paid forward" the support he received by providing Mr. John with the encouragement he needed to pursue investing in stocks. If not for him, it may have taken another 10 years before Mr. John found the courage to purchase his first share of stock. Think of the amount of reinvested dividends and compounded interest he would have lost out on! I believe that's why it's so important to expose others to the world of investing.

After spending several years in the investment industry, I realized that so many people sat on the outside and looked in. When I began my career, I concentrated my energies on prospecting high net-worth clients who had assets of at least $100,000. I recall presenting a seminar to our existing high net-worth customers and their friends at an exclusive hotel in San Francisco. When I scanned the audience, I realized that the attendees didn't need more information on how to invest. They were already wealthy and clearly had mastered the principles of investing. They were taking advantage of the elaborate hors d'oeuvres and using these events to network with their peers.

I decided that the people who needed the most help were not privy to this exclusive event. That's why I created a radio show targeting average Americans, focusing my energies on investment education. However, Mr. John showed me that people need more than information. They need someone to take them by the hand and show them how to get started. They need to be brought "inside" and shown exactly what to do.

Get Others Started in Investing

Mr. John took "pay it forward" to a new level the day he offered to transfer one share at a time of a stock that he owns into the names of radio listeners so they can experience what it means to own stock. Frankly, I was really concerned about his approach. It seemed simple to transfer shares of a stock and have people reimburse the costs, but the paperwork could be complicated. He told me he was doing this to calm new investors' fears and get them started, saying, "Ms. Debbie, people need more than lip service—they need help." Once they received the share, they could enroll in the dividend reinvestment program and watch their shares accumulate. He suggested they also show people in their close circle how easy and sensible it is to invest. This showed Mr. John's generosity and abundant mindset.

The fact that he was an experienced and successful investor provided a tremendous amount of confidence to potential investors who listened to my program. More than that, it increased their comfort level. Of course, the share he transferred was of a large, well-known blue chip company; he told them to only risk money they could afford to lose—the same advice his mentor had given him before he purchased his first shares stock. Once again, Mr. John had made an astute observation, which I am simply passing on. Pay it forward.

Pay It Forward to Your Children

Remember in my initial review of Mr. John's portfolio, I listed several accounts that were in the names of his three children? He had invested in stocks and mutual funds for his children, opening IRAs for them. This is a great place to start.

I suggest the first place to "pay it forward" is to your children. They have the most important asset of all—time. In addition, they can experience "how money works" before they leave your household. I think this is the greatest gift that any parent can give their offspring. In addition, investing in a college savings plan for your children early—in fact, when they are born —can mean the difference between them attending the college of their choice or having to contend with debt from college loans.

Instead of piling the latest electronic games or designer clothing under the Christmas tree, give each of your children a share of stock from a company that makes their favorite gadget. (You can print off an actual certificate at www.oneshare.com or visit www.yahoo.com/finance and research public companies.) Better yet, have your child do the research and determine if the latest fad indeed comes from a profitable enterprise. Being creative and "paying it forward" may produce a budding investment guru like the famous billionaire Warren Buffet.

Distribute Stocks as Gifts

"Paying it forward" can also be used to distribute

gifts to your closest friends and colleagues. Graduations, weddings, birthdays, and childbirth can provide great opportunities. An "old school" gift was buying a savings bond for nieces and nephews on their birthdays. The "new school" approach is giving them the gift of a share of stock or mutual funds.

Years ago, buying stock was a cumbersome process. Now, most companies allow buyers to establish accounts and purchase shares to gift to someone else online. The fee to register stock is minimal and enrolling in direct stock investment programs has never been easier. For example, Home Depot allows people to invest in their stock by visiting their website. How's that for do-it-yourself?

You can enroll in dividend reinvestment programs and direct stock investment programs by contacting the appropriate transfer agent. The "Value Line Investment Survey" or "Standard and Poor Research" information at your local library can provide you with the telephone number and address of organizations that administer their programs, usually a bank or company that specializes in managing shareholder services.

Paying a Home Forward

When my husband and I were first married, we had to start from an asset base of almost zero. But we were fortunate enough to purchase my mother-in-law's co-op town home when she decided to move into a senior citizen housing complex. It was in an excellent location and conveniently located next to the senior citizen apartment building she moved into. I believe she moved out because it was her one asset that she could pass on to her son.

Her co-op housing arrangement did not allow her to accumulate equity at the same rate as a conventional mortgage. As a result, my mother-in-law didn't receive much of a payout; much of the monthly co-op payment was applied to the maintenance of the units and surrounding areas. Yet, the value of her gift is immeasurable as she "paid forward" a home. Simply transferring the ownership to us meant we didn't have to pay rent or to come up with a down payment to buy.

Establish a Will

After conducting the portfolio review, I encouraged Mr. John to make a full account of his investments and establish a will. He didn't fully know how much he had invested and quickly realized it would be extremely difficult for his wife to know it, either. The current values of his assets weren't enough to be assessed estate taxes, but if they continued to grow, his estate might be subject to taxes in the future.

When people die without a will, the results of years of sweat and effort rarely get distributed properly and may go unaccounted for. It's best to put our financial houses in order so we can decide how to pay our assets forward at the time of our deaths. We should have a "last will and testament" filed away with our personal papers and copies held in a safe-deposit box outside of our home where they can't be destroyed prematurely. No one wants to talk about death, but let's face it: This is the only event that is guaranteed. Preparing a will simply provides another opportunity to "pay it forward" to the next generation.

Truly Self-Made?

I often hear people talk on and on about how they are self-made. But I believe it's not possible to be a "self-

It doesn't matter how much you earn today or whether you went to college or finished high school. Mr. John is living proof that you can build wealth on any income. You don't have to have an MBA in finance or earn six figures. The only possible obstacle is not believing that you have what it takes to "nickel and dime" your way to wealth. It's not hard, but it ain't easy.

made" anything. If we've experienced success, it's the result of someone "paying it forward." Even Mr. John had a co-worker who encouraged him to invest. He didn't make any assumptions about his ability to understand investing or whether he could afford it. Indeed, he knew he couldn't afford *not* to.

Mr. John is an extraordinary human being and continues to affect my life and countless others. I've learned more from this humble, generous man about investing than an MBA in finance could ever teach. His life validated the path that I chose in my quest to inspire others to build wealth. His story is my way of "paying it forward."

Pass it on!

<u>Common Cents #7</u>

<u>Pay It Forward</u>

Success leaves footprints

Share your good fortune

with others.

A Quick Review

Let's review the seven principles learned through this book:

1. Outlook Determines Outcome: Make sure you have the right outlook on your finances. Your outlook really does determine your outcome. With the right outlook, you can respond to life's adversities with courage. Because the economy is cyclical, the stock market goes up and down. How you respond to negative changes will determine your ultimate success. Having the right attitude and expecting positive outcomes will help you to stay the course.

2. How Money Works: Understanding how money works is essential to achieving your financial goals. Making a commitment to "put something away from every pay" helped Mr. John develop the right mindset. After learning how to manage his earnings, he was able to purchase a home and develop an enterprise, which allowed him to put part of his money at risk without jeopardizing his financial stability. Mr. John had developed a solid financial foundation prior to investing in stock. After he made his investment in stocks, he was able to compare their performance to his savings' meager accumulation. Watching his shares grow through reinvestment, automatic account builders, and employee stock purchase program provided firsthand experience in "how money works." You cannot gain investment experience while sitting on the sidelines. Do whatever is necessary to get in—and then stay in—the game.

3. Dream Big! Act Small!: One of the greatest lessons I learned from Mr. John is "the power of one." Dream big! Act small! It took a while for me to understand how investing in just one share of stock can be so powerful. Adding nickel and dimes, and reinvesting dividends, creates momentum. Acting small is the greatest advice I can give you. It means you don't have to wait to come up with $2,500 to meet most mutual fund minimums because most investment companies will reduce those minimums to $50 a month if you act small. If you want to purchase one share of stock, many companies will allow you to invest directly without any minimums. (Visit www.netstockdirect.com)

4. You Have What You Need: You'll find that investing isn't all that complicated as you begin to learn more about it. You don't have to buy in to common excuses like "Investing is too complicated," or "I don't have the money to invest." To "find money," scrutinize your spending behavior and find ways to redirect your money. Simply change a habit like buying magazines every week or coffee every day, and redirect the money you didn't spend to savings. The level of sacrifice you make depends on how badly you want your dream. You can start now.

5. Set It and Forget It: Too much information or "noise" can be hazardous to your wealth. Checking your investments minute by minute and responding to every economic news announcement can hinder your progress. Keep abreast of economic trends and review your quarterly investment statements to monitor your investment performance. Remember, it's not about how much, it's about for how long. If you try to time your investments thinking that will give you a strategic advantage, you'll probably make the wrong moves. Look at the evidence. Even professional investment managers with analytical tools and years of experience have proven unsuccessful at timing the market. Just set it and forget it. This approach has worked for Mr. John and thousands of other investors. Don't ignore your investments, but allow time for them to work in your favor.

6. It's Never Too Late: When Mr. John found the courage to ask a broker for advice in the parking lot, he discovered that building wealth is a team sport. You can create your own parking lot! Remember, you already have what you need. To learn how money works, become a student—attend seminars and ask for advice.

Free seminars provide great opportunities to interact with financial advisors and establish relationships. Also, subscribe to personal finance magazines and keep abreast of market activity. Once you begin to understand the language, you'll feel more confident asking questions and applying financial concepts to your unique situation. Knowledge is power.

7. Pay It Forward: People need someone to take them by the hand and show them how to get started. You can take your knowledge and experience and "pay it forward" to your family and friends. Teach them about how money works so they can benefit from the magic of compounding interest for as long as possible. Consider giving shares of stocks as gifts, or passing on your home. And establish a will to make the final decision of how your assets are ultimately paid forward.

ABOUT THE AUTHOR

Deborah Owens feels passionate about helping people of all incomes build wealth. Through her books, radio show, and public speaking tours, she inspires listeners with stories of real people achieving extraordinary results. A sought-after speaker at conferences throughout the nation, she encourages people to "dream big and act small" and shows them how to do it!

Deborah is president of Owens Media Group LLC, which creates customized sales training and financial empowerment programs for Fortune 500 companies. Visit her website at www.deborahowens.com for more information.

Breinigsville, PA USA
02 March 2011
256767BV00001B/1/A